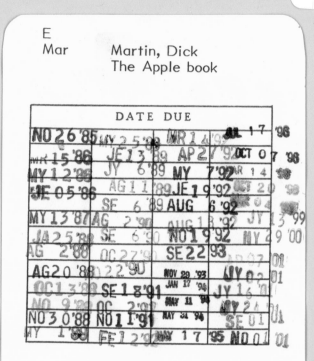

The Apple Book

Story and Pictures
by Dick Martin

GOLDEN PRESS • NEW YORK
Western Publishing Company, Inc.
Racine, Wisconsin

1977 GOLDENCRAFT® Edition

Apples grow on apple trees. An apple is a kind of fruit.

At our house we like all kinds of fruit.

We like grapes. Grapes grow on vines.

We like yellow cherries and purple cherries,

and red cherries baked in a pie.

We like blueberries

and strawberries

BERRIES

and blackberries.

Pears are shiny
and smooth.

Peaches and apricots are fuzzy and soft.

(They are all juicy
and sweet.)

The bananas we eat
grow in warm
and sunny places.

The prickly pineapple
is a tropical fruit.

Our favorite melon is watermelon.

Nuts are fruits that have hard shells.

A tomato is a fruit, too. Did you know that?